Using Picture Books to Help Little Ones Learn About Themselves

By Gayle Bentley and Lin Lim
Edited by Lisa Sticca-Conrod, JD, MS

Published by GHF Press
A Division of Gifted Homeschoolers Forum

Copyright © 2023 GHF Press

No part of this book may be reproduced or transmitted in any form or by any means, electronic or mechanical, including photocopying, recording, or by any information storage and retrieval system, without the written permission from the publisher.

Because of the dynamic nature of the Internet, any web addresses or links contained in this book may have changed since publication and may no longer be valid. The views expressed in this work are solely those of the author and do not necessarily reflect the views of the publisher, and the publisher hereby disclaims any responsibility for them. All rights reserved.

ISBN: 978-1-7375161-3-2
eBook ISBN: 978-1-7375161-4-9

Printed in the United States of America

J., W., C., & S. - Thank you for your love and support.
E.G. - Thank you for always listening.
R.Q. - You are why teachers teach.
~G.B.

To my family,
for the priceless gift of embracing who we are
and the acceptance of others.
~L.L

Table of Contents

Introduction

1. Why Is It So Important That I Read with My Child?... 10

2. What If My Child Seems Different?... 15

3. How Do I Bring Out the Best in My Child?... 26

4. How Do I Help My Child Accept Themselves and Accept Others?................ 36

5. How Do I Build Empathy in My Child?... 54

6. How Do I Calm My Worried Child?... 63

7. What if My Child Is a Perfectionist?... 77

8. How Do I View My Child as a Whole Person?... 89

Important Terms... 93

Introduction

"The best gift anyone can give, I believe, is the gift of sharing themselves."
~ Oprah Winfrey

Purpose

The purpose of this book is to encourage you to read (or continue reading) daily with your young child, and to help you select excellent picture books that address certain things you may notice in your child. Not only will these high-quality books have creative stories and interesting characters, but those characters may be people (or animals) with whom your child can relate. While your child enjoys the story, you will be presented with a golden opportunity to discuss tricky topics, such as empathy or perfectionism, as these issues are illustrated through the characters' adventures.

We include a number of sensitive topics in this resource of picture books, such as leading with strengths, accepting differences in ourselves and others, building empathy, addressing worry, and managing perfectionism. We also discuss viewing your child as a whole person and not exclusively through the lens of their abilities or disabilities. Each topic will be described in terms of behaviors you (or others) may see in your child. A research-based perspective will be given, followed by a list of books with their respective synopses and why your child would enjoy each book.

The topics we selected through our choices of picture books will be beneficial to all children but particularly apropos for gifted or twice-exceptional (2e) children. Gifted children typically learn more quickly, demand more complexity, and often sail past their same-age peers in the classroom. Children who are 2e share these same gifted characteristics but also have an accompanying disability, such as dyslexia or autism, which can add challenges to their academic as well as their social and emotional learning.

"One purpose of this book is to empower parents to help their child from an early age, make them more self-aware of their perceived differences, and learn how to make their differences "work" for them."

When parents notice their child is learning or behaving differently from other children, they may view them with concern. Each specialist will view your child through their own lens, often looking for what is "wrong." This is referred to as a **deficits-based approach**. As a result, children can be mislabeled, leading to poor treatment plans and confusion on the part of the parent. The main goal of this approach is to find perceived weaknesses in your child, and then work to "fix" them. Why is this a problem? Speaking from experience, it is discouraging and often demotivating to hear only what is "wrong" with your child and not what is "right." One purpose of this book is to empower parents to help their child from an early age, to make them more self-aware of their perceived differences, and to learn how to make their differences "work" for them.

As such, we wrote this book from the alternative **strength-based perspective** that helps children find their strengths and interests, provides opportunities to work in these areas, and uses strengths and interests as an entryway to practice skills needed to succeed in life[1]. Every child learns and develops at their own rate and in their own way. No two children follow the same path. For example, my (Lin) daughter, who is profoundly gifted, has many interests and is willing to pursue any number of them at any given time. However, my son, in stark contrast, is a 'just-in-time' learner. This is a term I coined to describe learners who actively seek needed skills for immediate use within their current area of interest. That is to say, he was only interested in learning what he needed to know at that moment. Developmentally, some children have more difficulty working toward a long-term goal than an immediate one, and need to focus on one thing at a time. Therefore, if this is the case, we should use their current areas of interest to increase their willingness to work through identified challenges.

---

1 Baum, S., Schader, R., & Owen, S. (2017). *To be gifted and learning disabled: Strength-based strategies for helping twice-exceptional students with LD, ADHD, ASD and more (3rd Ed.)*. Routledge.

For example, I (Gayle) utilized a strength-based strategy to help a child complete a dreaded writing task. I worked with a 2e elementary-aged boy who was very passionate about the impacts of climate change. He worried about the implications for the animals in the Arctic as the icebergs continue to melt. Because writing was a non-preferred task for this student, the teacher often struggled to find ways to encourage him to finish his writing assignments. I suggested the student create a presentation informing others about his concerns for Arctic animals. He willingly filled his poster with important information and was excited to present it to his class. Ta-da! The boy practiced his writing (and presentation) skills because he was enthused about the topic. Mission accomplished!

Why We Wrote This Book

    We wrote this book as a resource for parents with young children who may notice differences in their child's development or behavior that vary from what might be expected. Through our combined 50-plus years of experience as educators, scholars, and parents of neurodivergent children, we realized the importance of parents having early conversations about strengths and differences to build skills for healthy mental growth in our young children. Rather than ask busy parents to do *one more thing*, we believe that shared reading time with your child is a place where you can address difficult or uncomfortable topics. We have selected over forty excellent picture books to help you.

    I (Gayle) have spent many years teaching music to thousands of students in the public schools. I have taught children from Pre-K through 12th, from general music to high school orchestra. What I love about teaching music to the younger ones is that I have the opportunity to introduce them to beautiful pieces of music through listening, moving, singing, and performing on instruments. What I love about teaching older music students is that they have identified music as an interest (and often a strength) and want to become more advanced musicians. Because musical abilities vary from student to student, I work with students individually as often as possible, getting to know each one's strengths, making suggestions to improve weaknesses, and encouraging them to be the best they can be. My husband and I follow the same philosophy as the parents of our three neurodivergent sons. Each one has incredible abilities with challenges along the way. Our job is to help them discover their strengths and interests while providing the scaffolding or support when needed.

Over the years, I have advocated for gifted and twice-exceptional students in the schools where I have taught. To reach more teachers and parents in the community, I pursued my doctorate in cognitive diversity in education. I hope this book will benefit the many parents of gifted and 2e children who feel unsure as they begin this journey.

Before I (Lin) had children, I earned a doctorate in Human Development Psychology. Little did I know I would soon be conducting my own research at home as a parent of two outlier children. **Outliers** include those with high abilities, challenges, or a combination of both in one or more areas. When I began my parenting journey 17 years ago, first with my daughter and then my son, I quickly noticed that my children were very different from each other and completely unlike the parenting books I had read. These differences, combined with my academic and research training, have helped me to critically assess current theories on human development and their real-world application (or lack thereof) for outliers such as gifted and 2e people. Our educational system is built to serve the majority of students but not outliers.

My struggles to help well-meaning educators and administrators understand the complex needs of my profoundly gifted and 2e minority children led me to delve into the educational field myself. My children have experienced a variety of educational environments over the past ten years - from public to private to homeschooling, community college classes, and even a residential university program. Despite my children's differences, they are experiencing success while maintaining their well-being because we have emphasized their strengths, supported their challenges, and, most importantly, approached our parenting holistically, as discussed in Chapter Eight. Like Gayle, I continue to serve as an advocate and spokesperson to bridge families, educators, and professionals from other fields to support diverse people's health and well-being.

Why Is It So Important That I Read with My Child?

"One of the greatest gifts adults can give - to their offspring and to their society - is to read to children." ~ Carl Sagan

Most parents agree that reading regularly to their young children is important. On those busy nights when we just want to get our children into bed so we can take a breath, we may skip our reading routine. Let's look at some research on maintaining a reading habit to see how important it is and what the actual benefits are for your kids.

A recent study[2] suggested that the earlier in life a child is read to, the more frequently the parents will engage in reading with the child. Good reading habits should start early with the parents, even before their babies are six months old! These same "early

---

2 Niklas, F., Cohrssen, C., & Tayler, C. (2016). The sooner, the better: Early reading to children. *SAGE Open*, 6(4). doi.org/10.1177/2158244016672715

readers" demonstrated higher levels of language development as they grew. We, of course, want our children to learn to read well. Little did we know that early reading habits also contribute to our children's speaking ability.

> *"Beyond academic benefits, reading can strengthen relationships between parents and their children."*

Another set of researchers[3] found that children who are read to as preschoolers and have access to many books in the home are more likely to read for pleasure in their later elementary years. As a parent of older children and an avid reader myself, I (Gayle) believe it is very important for my boys to spend time reading for learning and relaxation. Happily, I began those early reading habits with them many years ago.

Beyond academic benefits, reading can strengthen relationships between parents and their children. A survey was performed with parents

[3] McNally, S., Leech, K., Corriveau, K., & Daly, M. (2023). Indirect effects of early shared reading and access to books on reading vocabulary in middle childhood, *Scientific Studies of Reading*, DOI: 10.1080/10888438.2023.2220846

of elementary children, and they rated "enjoying books" and "bonding with child" equally and as the most important of five goals at each grade level[4]. Researchers have also found that when parents and children read together, it benefits *both* parents[5] and children[6], and it is associated with a lower risk for social-emotional concerns in young children[7].

Reading with your child can also be a safe co-regulation activity, allowing the child to adopt the parent's emotional stability. When parents and other trusted adults, such as teachers, read books to young children, this feeling of safety can help them co-regulate at home or school. Co-regulation can lead to self-regulation, which is managing one's thoughts and feelings to achieve personal goals. As children work to develop self-regulation, research has found they are more likely

[4] Audet, D., Evans, M. A., Williamson, K., & Reynolds, K. (2008). Shared book reading: Parental goals across the primary grades and goal-behavior relationships in junior kindergarten. *Early Education and Development*, 19(1), 112–137. doi.org/10.1080/10409280701839189
[5] Canfield, Miller, E. B., Shaw, D. S., Morris, P., Alonso, A., & Mendelsohn, A. L. (2020). Beyond language: Impacts of shared reading on parenting stress and early parent-child relational health. *Developmental Psychology*, 56(7), 1305–1315. doi.org/10.1037/dev0000940
[6-7] Martin, K., Beck, A. F., Xu, Y., Szumlas, G. A., Hutton, J. S., Crosh, C. C., & Copeland, K. A. (2022). Shared reading and risk of social-emotional problems. *Pediatrics (Evanston)*, 149(1), 1–. doi.org/10.1542/peds.2020-034876

to develop positive prosocial skills and have more enjoyable interactions with others[8].

Reading with your child doesn't necessarily stop at any particular age, especially with the gifted and 2e populations. We expect to read to our young children before they have learned to read independently, but what if your ten-year-old still wants to read with you? Don't be alarmed or annoyed; they just want to spend some quiet time with you or may even need to work through thoughts or emotions that they do not know how to express. It may be helpful to view reading as one of numerous opportunities for you to connect and bond with your children[9] even as they grow older and become more independent.

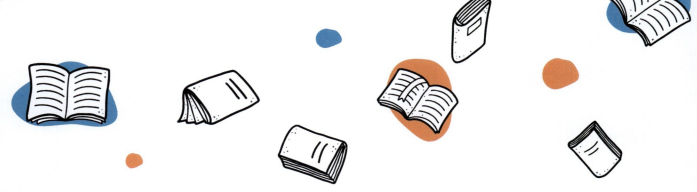

8 Rosanbalm, K.D., & Murray, D.W. (2017). *Caregiver co-regulation across development: A practice brief*. OPRE Brief #2017-80. Washington, DC: Office of Planning, Research, and Evaluation, Administration for Children and Families, US. Department of Health and Human Services.
9 World Literacy Foundation. (2021, November 26). *Bonding with your newborn through reading books*. worldliteracyfoundation.org/bonding-with-your-newborn-through-reading-books/

Reading with your child in a cozy, safe environment can help regulate stress levels - yours and theirs. The comforting sound of your voice and the feel of a gentle hug can serve as a positive sensory experience that improves your child's mood as well as their future ability to learn. Enjoy your time reading together as the days go by slowly, but the years will fly!

What If My Child Seems Different?

"It is time for parents to teach young people early on that in diversity there is beauty and there is strength." ~ Maya Angelou

In many ways, *sameness* is celebrated among humans. Children of the same age are placed in the *same* grade level at school, where they are taught the *same* material, regardless of ability. We tend to speak the *same* language and hold similar societal values as those around us. We all share the *same* human need for shelter, food, and comfort[10].

When we first learn that we are expecting a child, many of us read the same parenting books[11] to prepare us for what to expect. What if our child does not follow the month-by-month development guide or begins to exhibit some quirks that do not align with what we see in our best friend's child? What if we take our child to the park and he does not play with the other kids, instead opting

---

10 Maslow, A. H. (1943). A theory of human motivation. *Psychological Review*, 50(4), 370-396. doi.org/10.1037/h0054346
11 Murkoff, H. (2016). *What to expect when you're expecting (5th Ed.)*. Workman Publishing Company.

to draw planets with sidewalk chalk or regale the other moms with fun facts about fire trucks? Let's celebrate the differences in our children! The child who incessantly draws planets may grow up to become an astrophysicist. The fire truck "expert" might someday engineer new models for fire prevention. It is important to allow our children the freedom to be themselves and for us to reassure them that it is okay to be different.

"Our job as parents is to provide our children with opportunities to develop their potential as best we can. We want to create a setting of safety and security within our home and encourage exploration as our children grow."

Although our current society values sameness, there are signs that we are beginning to accept, appreciate, and celebrate the strengths that diversity brings to our world. Consider this idea during the ancient times of cave people. Cavemen would not have survived without some strategic, high-energy hunters and patient sorters and gatherers. Visual-spatial cave people helped design structures when they grew tired of living in caves. Cave people interested in music found time to sing and play using basic drums and carved bone flutes. Even artistic cave dwellers expressed their talent by painting on cave walls! We need humans with diverse interests and talents to make our world a more interesting and productive place.

Returning to our discussion about our own families, all children will learn and grow at different rates. When our child develops outside the expected timeframe, we may start to worry. Our job as parents is to provide our children with opportunities to develop their potential as best we can. We want to create a setting of safety and security within our home and encourage exploration as our children grow. If we notice areas of concern with our young children, addressing them as early as possible is best when we have the resources.

Examples of differences you may notice:

Asynchronous development

Advanced or unusual interests for their age

Higher (or lower) energy level than others

Intense feelings or reactions when compared to others

Preference for talking to adults rather than children

Differences in sleep patterns

Picky eating due to textures, smells, colors, or other food characteristics

Variances in the ability to tolerate frustrating situations

Sensitivity to textures such as shirt tags, socks, or certain clothing materials

Sensitivities to certain types of sounds or lighting (such as fluorescent)

This list of differences may seem familiar to you and/or your gifted or 2e children, or it may seem surprising or unusual. For gifted children and particularly 2e children and adults, it is quite common to have **sensory differences**, which means that their five senses respond differently to external stimuli than you might expect. Individual senses can be heightened or dampened depending on the person or situation. For example, a particular sound, like a bell, may be excruciatingly loud for one child while another finds the tag on the back of their shirt itchy. My (Gayle) oldest son refused to eat dinner in the kitchen of our new house until we changed the location of the trashcan because he said the smell was unbearable. (We did not smell anything out of the ordinary.)

Other points to consider about the gifted and 2e population include feeling emotions more strongly than expected, sleeping or energy level differences, and **asynchronous development**. Asynchronous development means that a child may be more developed in some ways and less in others. For example, a 10-year-old child might have the math skills of a high school student, the writing skills of a fifth grader, and the social and emotional skills of a 7-year-old - all in one person! It is a lot for them (and you) to understand sometimes because their behaviors will change depending on the situation. Regardless of the differences that you may notice in your child, having a strong parent-child relationship will serve as a buffer in times of stress, and reading together is an important way to promote this closeness. Read early and often to maximize the benefits.

Now, consider your child's experience when you are reading together. Do you appear to be engaged and invested in the main character's journey, or are you side-eyeing your phone for that text from work? Imagine how much more your child will benefit from your time together as you make thought-provoking comments about the pictures and respond to your child's curiosity. You do not need a degree in theater performance to be an engaging reader, but your child will know when you are not paying attention to the task at hand. Even my Goldendoodle gives up asking for cuddles when I pull out my phone. They know!

> *"You do not need a degree in theater performance to be an engaging reader, but your child will know when you are not paying attention to the task at hand."*

12 Muhinyi, A., Heskethm A., Stewart, A., & Rowland, C. (2020). Story choice matters for caregiver extra-textual talk during shared reading with preschoolers. *Journal of Child Language*, 47(3), 633-654. hgv10qduhp-mp02-y-https-doi-org.proxy.lirn.net/10.1017/S0305000919000783

We also want to consider which stories we choose when reading with our children. Recent research suggests preschoolers are more engaged and ask more complicated questions when a story is more complex[12]. Of course, our picture book choices should be high-quality and age-appropriate, but if your child can understand more complexity, try it. You will be able to determine your children's engagement level quickly enough if they are asking for a different book or leaving the scene altogether. A child's level of comprehension will often be higher than their reading level, so don't be afraid to read stories, even chapter books, together that they are not yet able to read alone.

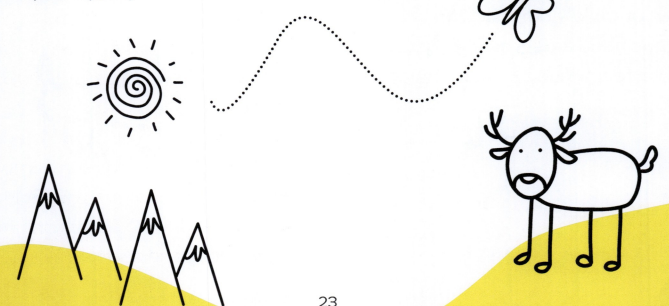

Tips to Grow On

Make daily reading a habit with your child. You will strengthen your bond and help with brain development, academic skills, and more. Plus, you are encouraging them to be lifelong readers.

Younger children may be ready to hear books with more advanced concepts, and that's okay. Their comprehension is often more advanced than their independent reading level at this stage. But be ready to answer lots of questions!

Your older children may still enjoy reading with you, and that's okay. They might need quality reading time together before bed as they spend more time at school and less time with you during the day.

Be in the moment when you are reading with your child. Turn off your phone and enjoy this fleeting time.

Worth Noting

As we wrote this book, we discovered that a significant number of children's picture books could be found on YouTube as read-alouds. It can be expensive to buy a library's worth of books as your children grow, so this is an opportunity for you to see the books and hear the stories online before you buy. It is also a great way to continue your nightly storytime while traveling. All you need is access to the internet. Have fun!

How Do I Bring Out the Best in My Child?

"If a child is poor in math but good at tennis, most people would hire a math tutor. I would rather hire a tennis coach." ~ Deepak Chopra

All of us want the best for our children. How do we bring out their best, particularly if we notice differences in their development or behavior? We allow them to try many things, find what they enjoy, and make sure they have the chance to do those things frequently. Maybe your child is overly sensitive, energetic, or inattentive compared to same-age peers. Maybe your child has meltdowns or anxiously avoids meeting new people. Should remediating challenging behaviors be our primary emphasis as we raise our young children, or have you forgotten that your little one has the voice of an angel, the touch of an artist, or the mind of an architect? Let's lead our children to work in their areas of strength while we help to support their challenges.

Think of a sport, an activity, or a subject in school that you have tried but did not enjoy. I (Gayle) recall a story my father once shared with me. He is a retired physicist and one of the most intelligent people I know. He was required to take three years of a foreign language in high school and chose German. In his first year, he earned an A, the second year a B, and the third a C. He finished his linguistic career, sure that he would have failed had he continued. Despite his high intelligence, learning languages was not an interest. Imagine that my dad was not allowed to study physics but instead sent to a school to study linguistics. All day long, he was taught to speak and read in multiple languages. Despite his other strengths and interests (e.g., math, science, and music), he would have felt like a failure if his success had been measured only by his ability to work with language. His weaknesses would have been emphasized instead of allowing him to lead with his many strengths.

> "Let's lead our children to work in their areas of strength while we help to support their challenges."

Leading with strengths and interests helps children feel more confident and successful. When they enjoy what they are doing, they will be more open to input from others. They will likely be in a better mood, and you will see fewer behavioral challenges. I (Gayle) often advise teachers about adapting class activities for gifted and 2e students. By this, I mean tweaking an assignment to appeal to a particular child's interests. Although this seems like more work for a teacher, an engaged student causes fewer interruptions because they are no longer bored. This is true at home and in other places as well. If you have the option of signing your inattentive child up for a preferred 2-hour robotics class or a non-preferred 1-hour writing class, choose robotics and watch the time evaporate!

Now, you may be wondering, do I always choose the activity my child prefers? How will children strengthen their weaker academic skills if they are not practiced? We can use domains of interest and strength to bridge to areas of challenge[13]. For example, suppose a child who is a struggling reader is fascinated by black holes. In that case, you might search for books about black holes at their reading level for independent reading. A child is significantly more likely to read if they have access to books that interest them. Another alternative would be to provide books of interest with higher complexity and read aloud to your child.

Researchers have recently found that listening to a book activates the same parts of the brain as reading the book ourselves[14]. As your child gets older, the reading demands will increase at school, and fortunately, it is easy to find textbooks and novels in audiobook formats. With the number of good books accessible at libraries and online, we should be able to match our children's interests (and accommodations) with high-quality literature.

---

13 Baum, S., Schader, R., & Owen, S. (2017). *To be gifted and learning disabled: Strength-based strategies for helping twice-exceptional students with LD, ADHD, ASD and more (3rd Ed.)*. Routledge.

14 Deniz, F., Nunez-Elizalde, A. O., Huth, A. G., & Gallant, J. L. (2019). The representation of semantic information across human cerebral cortex during listening versus reading is invariant to stimulus modality. *The Journal of Neuroscience, 39(39)*, 7722–7736. doi.org/10.1523/JNEUROSCI.0675-19.2019

As you discover your child's many strengths and interests over time, you will enjoy your parenting journey even more. Celebrating their joy with them as they learn and grow is fun. We have selected the books below because many of the characters worry because their strengths and interests differ from those around them. They become the heroes of their stories when they use their talents to overcome challenges or solve problems. As you share these stories with your child, you can discuss your strengths and help them discover theirs.

"They become the heroes of their stories when they use their talents to overcome challenges or solve problems."

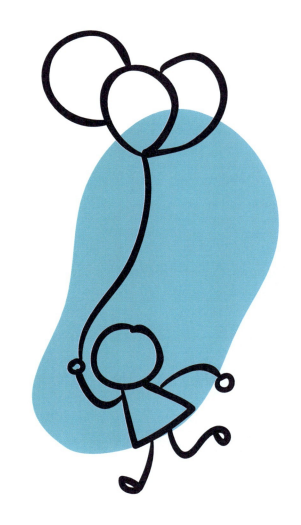

Tips to Grow On

Encourage children to work in areas of interest frequently. They will be happier, better behaved, and more productive.

Working with topics of interest can motivate your child to do hard things (e.g., reading).

As you help your child find areas of interest and strength, you will feel more positive about being your child's parent, which will help you during the tough times.

Wonderful books can be found on almost any topic. Help your children find books that match their interests and discover new ones!

Suggested Books to Read About Leading with Strengths

Appelemando's Dreams
by Patricia Polacco (1991)

Key Issues: Leading with strengths, Accepting differences in others

Summary: Appelemando is a little boy who spends much of his time dreaming. The townspeople do not understand him, but he has four kind friends who believe in him. His gift is not accepted when he paints the town with pictures of his dreams. However, the townspeople proclaim him a hero when he saves his friends by using his gift.

Child Appeal: Wildly creative storytelling and illustrations

Aaron Slater, Illustrator
by Andrea Beaty (2021)

Key Issues: Leading with strengths

Summary: Iggy Peck has loved to draw and listen to stories since he was young. When it is time to learn to read, Iggy finds it very difficult. His second-grade teacher encourages him to tell stories through art while supporting him as he learns to read.

Child Appeal: Captivating rhymes, beautiful illustrations with multicultural characters

Ada Twist, Scientist
by Andrea Beaty (2016)

Key Issues: Leading with strengths

Summary: Ada does not speak until she turns three, but when she does, she is as curious as can be. She seeks answers to big questions everywhere she goes, and her parents tire of her experimentation. When they realize that her curiosity is a gift to be supported, Ada thrives and leads others to be curious, too.

Child Appeal: Captivating rhymes, beautiful illustrations with multicultural characters

C for Curiosity
by Lin Lim (2022)

Key Issues: Leading with strengths

Summary: This photo journey is a view through the lens of a cognitively diverse child. As we notice the similarities and differences in our perspectives, we can engage within a safe space and share our experiences in our areas of interest and strengths.

Child Appeal: Photos of Asian children, open-ended thoughts to discuss

Suggested Books to Read About Leading with Strengths

The Fantastic Bureau of Imagination
by Brad Montague (2023)

Key Issues: Leading with strengths

Summary: Special Agent Sparky loves to write poetry but is too afraid to share his work with others. One day, there is an explosion in the Cave of Untold Stories, and the word is spread that all need to share their creativity to save The Bureau. Sparky starts with his poetry, and others follow suit. The Fantastic Bureau of Imagination is saved, and everyone lives imaginatively ever after.

Child Appeal: Fantastically over-the-top tale with amazingly detailed pictures

Happy Dreamer
by Peter H. Reynolds (2018)

Key Issues: Leading with strengths, Accepting differences in yourself

Summary: There are dreamers of all sorts - happy ones, quiet ones, creative ones, and loud ones. You can truly be yourself when you follow your dreams, no matter your obstacles.

Child Appeal: Relatable story for daydreamers

Iggy Peck, Architect
by Andrea Beaty (2007)

Key Issues: Leading with strengths

Summary: Iggy Peck loves to design and build towers. He creates them everywhere he goes. When he gets to second grade, he is told that students do not spend time building in the classroom. School becomes quite dreary for Iggy until his unique skills are needed to save the day! Ultimately, he becomes the resident expert who teaches the other students about design and architecture.

Child Appeal: Engaging rhymes, beautiful illustrations

Sofia Valdez, Future Prez
by Andrea Beaty (2019)

Key Issues: Leading with strengths, Empathy

Summary: Sofia Valdez loves helping people. It is her superpower! When her grandfather hurts himself, tripping over trash while walking her to school, Sofia brings her town together to clean up the area and build a park for all to enjoy.

Child Appeal: Wonderful rhymes, beautiful illustrations with multicultural characters

How Do I Help My Child Accept Themselves and Accept Others?

"Be yourself; everyone else is already taken." ~ Oscar Wilde

Harvard Medical School defines **self-acceptance** as being aware of and accepting who we are, including *both* positive and negative[15] attributes. These include body acceptance, self-protection from negative criticism, and believing in one's abilities. Although self-acceptance and self-esteem are commonly used interchangeably, they are similar and interrelated but not identical[16]. Accepting ourselves is associated with our general mental well-being, while self-esteem is more closely related to positive feelings about ourselves. Self-acceptance is *internal*, as it comes from within, while positive feelings that build

---

[15] Pillay, S. (2016, May 16). *Greater self-acceptance improves emotional well-being.* Harvard Health Publishing. health.harvard.edu/blog/greater-self-acceptance-improves-emotional-well-201605169546

[16] Macinner, L. (2006). Self-esteem and self-acceptance: an examination into their relationship and their effect on psychological health. *Journal of Psychiatric and Mental Health Nursing, 13(5),* 483–489. doi.org/10.1111/j.1365-2850.2006.00959.x

self-esteem come from both outside (our interactions with the world) and inside us (how we feel about things). According to researchers, the benefits of self-acceptance included reports of higher life satisfaction[17] and a greater sense of well-being[18].

Of course, both are important and build upon each other! Accepting ourselves through non-judgment[19] prepares us to accept others and be available to build upon activities that make us feel good about ourselves (self-esteem). Cultural variations have been found in the effectiveness of different ways of supporting and building self-acceptance and self-esteem[20]. Consider our suggestions below to reflect on what resonates with you and your family.

17 Zipagan, F., & Galvez Tan, L. (2023). From self-compassion to life satisfaction: Examining the mediating effects of self-acceptance and meaning in life. *Mindfulness*, 14(9), 2145–2154. doi.org/10.1007/s12671-023-02183-8
18 Li, S., Zhang, X., Luo, C., Chen, M., Xie, X., Gong, F., Lv, F., Xu, J., Han, J., Fu, L., & Sun, Y. (2021). The mediating role of self-acceptance in the relationship between loneliness and subjective well-being among the elderly in nursing home: A cross-sectional study. *Medicine, 100(40)*, e27364. doi.org/10.1097/MD.0000000000027364
19 Chandna, S., Sharma, P., & Moosath, H. (2022). The mindful self: Exploring mindfulness in relation with self-esteem and self-efficacy in Indian population. *Psychological Studies, 67(2)*, 261–272. doi.org/10.1007/s12646-021-00636-5
20 Qian, Yu, X., & Liu, F. (2022). Comparison of two approaches to enhance self-esteem and self-acceptance in Chinese college students: Psychoeducational lecture vs. group Intervention. *Frontiers in Psychology, 13*, 877737–877737. doi.org/10.3389/fpsyg.2022.877737

"Remember that children's self-acceptance is often dictated by how we (adults) feel about ourselves."

Pairing self-acceptance with self-esteem-building opportunities

Your children will feel more accepting of themselves if taught to value what they have, not what they do not. We should start by accepting and appreciating what our bodies and minds can do, not simply how we look. Remember that children's self-acceptance is often dictated by how we (adults) feel about ourselves. For example, if we verbally criticize ourselves in the mirror, our child will learn to do the same. When our children are young, point out the fun activities that their bodies let them do. Then, we can remind our children to use and enjoy

their unique skills and talents. No one can do everything, but we can appreciate ourselves and others for what they can do! Teaching children to be grateful for their positive attributes will go a long way toward supporting children in times of stress or discontent.

Self-acceptance with gifted and 2e kids can be especially difficult - even with positive **role models** - because of their exceptionalities. However, by intentionally selecting and reading quality picture books, we can use the characters to send our young children positive messages about self-acceptance, as they are unlikely to accept others if they do not accept themselves first. We hope our children will be the next generation of people who will be more tolerant, kind, and accepting of others than previous generations. As such, we need literature to help us prepare our children for the complex world they face.

Providing positive role models for your children is another way to pair self-acceptance with self-esteem-building practices. A chosen positive role model can be a family member, a friend, or even a famous actor or athlete. Pointing out their struggles and how they overcame adversity becomes key in presenting the role model. Discuss their positive attributes and how developing their gifts helped them with their challenges. My (Gayle) friend's son, a swimmer, idolized Michael Phelps - both of whom have traits of hyper-focus and high energy. She and her son watched videos of his success and interviews with his coach, who discussed how Phelps used the traits of hyper-focus and high energy to help him become the greatest swimmer ever. My friend's son now had a "successful someone" with whom he could identify - in terms of interests and struggles - and then the voice in his head said, "If he can do it, so can I."

"When they help others, even in small ways, children will see that what they do makes a difference in the world."

Another way to encourage kids to feel good about themselves is to demonstrate *how* to help others. Giving examples through children's literature illustrating how *other children* take joy and derive satisfaction from helping others can inspire them to do the same. When they help others, even in small ways, children will see that what they do makes a difference in the world. Once they understand that helping others is a "good thing, " we can lead by example. With a young child, we can start by asking for help at home with age-appropriate chores. Having young children help gives them a sense of agency and a feeling of contribution as part of the family.

As they grow older, they will likely do community projects at school or can join after-school clubs, such as youth groups or scouts, perhaps collecting food for the homeless or cleaning up areas nearby. Of course, you can always create your own family project to help others in the community by working together at the local animal shelter or soup kitchen, which often helps them appreciate all that they *do* have. Helping others will make the whole family - especially the little ones - feel good and, hopefully, start a lifelong habit of service.

Accepting others

We use similarities and differences to classify objects, ideas, and events to make sense of our world. Even Sesame Street has a regular segment called "One Of These Things Is Not Like The Other." Let us help our children recognize and appreciate the differences that are found in the people of our community.

While society imposes many labels on people, it is important to teach our children that these classifications are not indicative of the whole of the person, whether it is themselves or someone else. Looking beyond the label and seeing people for who they are and for who they can become is imperative to their acceptance of themselves and others.

Approach these differences from a strength-based[21], positive[22] perspective that models our acceptance of ourselves. When we behave in a way that aligns with our beliefs, we will feel true to who we are, contributing positively to our mental health and well-being[23]. If a classmate has a physical disability, help your child think of everything they *can* do together. Your child will feel good helping a peer *and* increase their capacity to accept others. If a peer has a learning difference, invite your child to look for other interests and talents that the child possesses. We all have strengths AND challenges; everyone is unique, like snowflakes. If seen as an invitation to share and increase our knowledge of each other, our perception of differences can shift, and we can turn a negative experience into an opportunity for growth.

---

21 Barbre, J., & Anderson, I. (2022). *Supporting children's mental health and wellbeing: A strength-based approach for early childhood educators*. Redleaf Press.
22 Martin E. P. Seligman, Randal M. Ernst, Jane Gillham, Karen Reivich & Mark Linkins (2009). Positive education: positive psychology and classroom interventions, *Oxford Review of Education, 35(3)*, 293-311, DOI: 10.1080/03054980902934563
23 Klussman, K., Curtin, N., Langer, J., & Nichols, A. L. (2022). The importance of awareness, acceptance, and alignment with the self: A framework for understanding self-connection. *Europe's Journal of Psychology, 18(1)*, 120–131. doi.org/10.5964/ejop.3707

As in all things, we serve as powerful role models for our children[24]. We must ensure that we are modeling tolerance and kindness toward others, including those who may be different. Actions will indeed speak louder than words to our children. Additionally, encourage your children to ask questions about the differences they see in others. Let your child know that talking to you about these things is a good thing! Support your child if they seem afraid of differences in others. After discussing the differences they notice, challenge them to find similarities as well.

Teach your children how to meet others and ask them to join, avoiding exclusionary behaviors. This skill set is particularly useful if your child is shy by nature. Role-play at home with your child what they would say to someone new at the park or at school. Have them practice asking you to join a game until it feels natural to your child. Then, support your child to use these skills in real life, modeling patience if it takes more practice and time for your child to be comfortable and confident. You want your child to be a welcoming force among kids, not one who excludes others.

---

24 Obeldobel,C., & Kerns, K. A. (2021). A literature review of gratitude, parent–child relationships, and well-being in children. *Developmental Review, 61*, 100948–. doi.org/10.1016/j.dr.2021.100948

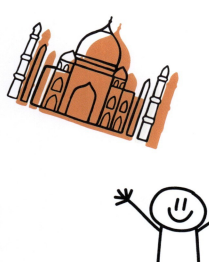

the traditions of holidays of different cultures and give one a try. Check out picture books or watch a children's show that celebrates the differences among various cultures. We have included a number of recommended picture books that show characters from other cultures to share with your child.

Show your children how *interesting* differences in people can be. Consider attending a community multicultural event where your children can enjoy other cultures' food, language, and performances. Explore

Tips to Grow On

 Children must learn to accept themselves in order to be accepting of others.

 We can teach our children to be more accepting of themselves and others through role modeling, helping others, and discussing differences and similarities with you.

 To help your child build self-esteem, use the strength-based strategies that we discussed in Chapter Three. When our children do things they love, they are more likely to experience success, making them feel more competent - equalling a solid boost of self-esteem.

 Introduce your children to different cultures through community events to widen their perspective of the world.

Suggested Books to Read About Accepting Differences

Agate
by Joy Morgan Dey and Nikki Johnson (2007)

Key Issues: Accepting yourself, Leading with strengths

Summary: Agate the Moose is convinced that his animal friends have many interesting talents and skills and that he has none. Each friend is named after a particular gem, from Opal to Diamond to Emerald. Agate feels brown and plain compared to the others. Agate's friends remind him that everyone is unique and that being yourself is the best way to feel happy.

Child Appeal: Beautifully painted pictures of animals; each animal identifies with a different gemstone

Awesomely Emma: A Charley and Emma Story
by Amy Webb (2020)

Key Issues: Accepting others

Summary: Emma has limb differences and uses a wheelchair, and when her friend Charley tries to do things for Emma on a school field trip, Emma feels upset. When Charley says he is trying to help because of her disability, she points out that everyone is different and that "no one can do everything that other people can do."

Child Appeal: We all struggle with something - no one is good at everything.

Suggested Books to Read About Accepting Differences

Be You!
by Peter H. Reynolds (2020)

Key Issues: Accepting yourself, Empathy, Leading with strengths

Summary: Be yourself, no matter what. Your differences and interests are what make you unique. Help others to choose their own paths.

Child Appeal: Wonderful illustrations, strong message

The Boy Who Grew Flowers
by Jen Wojtowicz (2005)

Key Issues: Accepting others, Leading with strengths

Summary: Rink Bowagon is a loner at school because he is different from the other students. A new student arrives who also has differences and is intrigued by Rink. They get to know one another, each celebrating what is different about the other, and they live happily ever after.

Child Appeal: Wonderful message, happily-ever-after ending

The Big Umbrella
by Amy June Bates (2018)

Key Issues: Accepting others

Summary: A kind-hearted red umbrella loves to shelter people and animals of all shapes, sizes, talents, and needs. As more come, the umbrella expands to include all.

Child Appeal: The personification of the umbrella is so heart-warming.

Busy Betty
by Reese Witherspoon (2022)

Key Issues: Accepting yourself, Leading with strengths

Summary: Betty is so busy that she is often reminded that to finish her work, she must focus. She decides to bathe her dog before her best friend arrives for a playdate, and Betty jumps from one thing to the next, creating a bigger and bigger mess! When her friend reframes the mess, Betty and her friend start a successful dog-washing business.

Child Appeal: Busy kids will relate to Betty's antics.

Suggested Books to Read About Accepting Differences

Eggbert: The Slightly Cracked Egg
by Tom Ross and Rex Barron (1994)

Key Issues: Accepting yourself, Accepting others, Leading with strengths

Summary: Eggbert is an egg who lives happily in a refrigerator with his friends until, one day, it is discovered that he has a crack. He is told to leave and searches for a new home. Despite his attempts to fit in, no one accepts Eggbert because of the crack. He decides that he does belong and uses his artistic talents to paint pictures of cracks found around the world.

Child Appeal: Demonstrates using strengths and the power of forgiveness

Giraffes Can't Dance
by Giles Andreae and Guy Parker-Rees (2001)

Key Issues: Accepting yourself, Accepting others

Summary: Gerald the Giraffe is good at certain things, but dancing is not one of them. The other animals laugh at his attempts. He sinks away in shame but meets a wise cricket who reminds him that it is okay to be different. When Gerald dances to his own tune, he is celebrated by all.

Child Appeal: Great rhymes, endearing characters

Moses Goes to a Concert
by Isaac Millman (1998)

Key Issues: Accepting others

Summary: Moses and his fellow deaf classmates go on a field trip to watch a deaf percussionist perform with an orchestra. The kids hold balloons so they can feel the vibrations, and the percussionist performs in socks so she can, too! After the concert, they meet with the percussionist, and Moses decides that he can be anything he wants if he works hard.

Child Appeal: Cool pictures of instruments of the orchestra, sign-language chart

Odd Velvet
by Mary E. Whitcomb (1998)

Key Issues: Accepting others, Leading with strengths

Summary: A little girl named Velvet is different from the other students at school. She collects rocks and plants and brings strange things for lunch. At first, her classmates ostracize her, but when she wins the art competition, they learn to respect her strengths and see her differences in a new way.

Child Appeal: Relatable characters

Suggested Books to Read About Accepting Differences

Red
by Michael Hall (2015)

Key Issues: Accepting yourself, Leading with strengths

Summary: Red the Crayon feels different. Whenever he is asked to draw things that should be red, like strawberries, they turn out blue. He feels like a failure until, one day, a new friend asks him to draw the ocean, and he does! Despite his label, Red realizes that he is a blue crayon, and when he focuses on creating what he draws well, he is happy and accepted.

Child Appeal: Creatively written metaphor

The Story of Ferdinand
by Munro Leaf (1936)

Key Issues: Accepting others

Summary: Ferdinand is a bull who is different from the others. Instead of running and playing, he sits under a tree, smelling the flowers all day. When he is mistakenly chosen for a bullfight in Madrid, Ferdinand sits in the ring and refuses to fight. He is returned to his home and happily revels in his uniqueness.

Child Appeal: Ferdinand's gentleness

When Charley Met Emma
by Amy Webb (2019)

Key Issues: Accepting yourself, Accepting others, Empathy

Summary: Charley sometimes feels different from his friends because he likes to sit and draw. At the park, he meets Emma, who has limb differences. At first, he is afraid, but Emma helps him realize that, while she may have physical differences, she and Charley also share many similarities.

Child Appeal: Authentic feelings, physical differences

When I Draw a Panda
by Amy June Bates (2020)

Key Issues: Accepting yourself, Leading with strengths

Summary: A little girl is an artist who loves to draw things her own way. She creates a panda who draws with her. She and her panda enjoy exploring their unique artistry, ignoring critiques from others.

Child Appeal: A must-read for little artists!

How Do I Build Empathy in My Child?

"If there is any one secret of success, it lies in the ability to get the other person's point of view and see things from his angle as well as your own."
~ Henry Ford

We all want our children to learn to show empathy toward others as they grow. Empathy is the ability to put ourselves in another person's shoes. Children are inherently self-interested (for survival purposes) when they are very young - their needs and desires come before the needs and desires of others. However, it is crucial to note that empathy, to some degree, is innate but needs to be cultivated by parental influence. In fact, parental empathy has a significant direct correlation with greater child empathy[25]. Over time, modeling empathy for children bears sweet fruit - the more empathy a parent shows for the child and others, the more empathetic a child becomes. No one book or

---

25 Hu, Y., Emery, H. T., Ravindran, N., & McElwain, N. L. (2020). Direct and indirect pathways from maternal and paternal empathy to young children's socioemotional functioning. *Journal of Family Psychology, 34*(7), 825–835. doi.org/10.1037/fam0000745

act can make anyone more empathetic necessarily, but planting the seed through literature and practice (both parent and child) helps to enrich the soil for the empathetic tree to take root.

As we lead our children to learn more about other people and how the world works, they will begin to view things from others' perspectives. Empathy has been listed as *the* most essential leadership skill[26] in business. However, it is a critical skill for any adult. If we were more empathetic as a society, there might be less bias, racism, and crime. Parental warmth, sensitivity, and strong parent-child relationships correlate positively to empathy[27].

26 Brower, T (2021, September 19). Empathy is the most important leadership skill according to research. *Forbes*. forbes.com/sites/tracybrower/2021/09/19/empathy-is-the-most-important-leadership-skill-according-to-research/?sh=121630ae3dc5
27 Spinrad, T., & Gal, D. E. (2018). Fostering prosocial behavior and empathy in young children. *Current Opinion in Psychology, 20*, 40–44. doi.org/10.1016/j.copsyc.2017.08.004

"Each time they hear the message, they will likely become more empathetic teenagers and, eventually, adults."

How do we help our self-interested little children transform into empathetic grownups who genuinely care for others? One way is for us to bond with our children in their early years by reading, playing, and snuggling together. Next, we model empathy through the natural course of our daily life. We show them what it looks like when we help a neighbor, attend a friend's parent's funeral, or visit a lonely nursing home resident. Also, we point out when we see others showing empathy. When a friend helps you, tell your child how much it means to you. Most importantly, praise your children when they express empathy for others. Each time they hear the message, they will likely become more empathetic teenagers and, eventually, adults.

The recommended books below give us beautiful stories demonstrating what empathetic characters do. They sit quietly. They acknowledge. They encourage. Many of the authors have paired empathy with having big feelings in life. Has your child ever cried because a small bug was squished or a friend was injured? Alternatively, your child may have difficulty *understanding* why others are upset. For little ones, empathy is much about learning to acknowledge and understand their own feelings. Then, we can help them notice and understand the feelings of others.

In *Adrian Simcox Does Not Have a Horse* by Marcy Campbell, a young girl cannot understand why a boy tells made-up stories about owning a horse. She spends her time disproving what the boy says until her mother walks her past his house in a poor neighborhood. When the girl sees the boy's challenges, she understands why he creates fantastical stories at school. This well-written story can stimulate several things to talk about with your child - the boy's motivation for storytelling, the girl's intention to prove him wrong, and the mother's wisdom in showing her the answer.

As you read these books with your children, you can use what the characters do (and do not do) to discuss the feelings and thoughts of others. Because your child feels safe and comfy with you and enjoys a good story, they will be more emotionally open to engage in a conversation about empathy. Children love repetition, so you may end up reading the story together several more times. Each re-reading will solidify the message further, just as you will continue to model empathy in your life.

Tips to Grow On

 Empathy is an important skill that can be taught through parent modeling and encouragement.

 Young children will need help understanding and acknowledging their own feelings. This will form the basis for them to understand the feelings of others.

 Gifted and 2e children often have big feelings and may feel more strongly about a situation than expected.

 When our children see empathetic characters in picture books, the characters can serve as role models and stimulate parent-child discussions about empathy.

Suggested Books to Read About Empathy

Adrian Simcox Does Not Have a Horse
by Marcy Campbell (2018)

Key Issues: Empathy, Accepting others

Summary: A young girl notices a lonely boy at school who talks about owning a horse. She is convinced this could not be true, as he lives in a small house with his grandfather. The girl's mother wisely takes her on a walk past the boy's house, and she learns to be more empathetic towards others who are different.

Child Appeal: Easily relatable journey of empathy

The Boy with Big, Big Feelings
by Britney Winn Lee (2019)

Key Issues: Empathy, Big feelings

Summary: A boy with big feelings worries that he is the only one who feels this way. He thinks he must hide these emotions until, one day, he meets a little girl with big feelings. They become friends and learn that big emotions affect others as well.

Child Appeal: It is comforting to know that others are like us.

Jenny Mei Is Sad
by Tracy Subisak (2021)

Key Issues: Empathy, Big feelings

Summary: A little girl notices that her friend, Jenny Mei, is sometimes sad. Jenny does not always show it on her face or say it in words, but her friend notices it in other ways. When Jenny has a hard day, her friend supports her because that is what friends do, even when things are difficult.

Child Appeal: Heartwarming feelings invoked through understanding, multicultural characters

The Many Colors of Harpreet Singh
by Supriya Kelkar (2019)

Key Issues: Empathy, Big feelings

Summary: Harpreet wears a special colored patka, or headpiece, every day, one that reflects his mood. He wears yellow when happy, pink to celebrate, and red when he needs courage. When he moves to a different part of the country, he wears white to seem invisible at his new school. Eventually, he meets a new friend and returns to his cheerful, colorful self.

Child Appeal: A charming multicultural perspective on the stress of moving to a new school

Suggested Books to Read About Empathy

Pocketful of Sads
by Brad Davidson (2023)

Key Issues: Empathy, Big feelings

Summary: Bear is sad and does not know why. Rabbit tries to "fix" his mood with happy thoughts, joke-telling, knitting, yoga, and painting, but nothing works! It turns out that Bear just needed some quiet time sitting with his friend.

Child Appeal: Shows that moods cannot always be fixed

The Rabbit Listened
by Cori Doerrfeld (2018)

Key Issues: Empathy, Big feelings

Summary: A young boy who is crushed when his block tower is knocked over is visited by his animal friends. Each suggests a different way to manage his emotions, from ignoring them to yelling to knocking down someone else's building. Only the rabbit listens quietly as the boy talks through his feelings and concludes what he must do to feel better.

Child Appeal: Realistic responses to frustration and the use of a rabbit to find calmness

How Do I Calm My Worried Child?

"Do not anticipate trouble, or worry about what may never happen. Keep in the sunlight." ~ Henry Ford

"Worry often gives a small thing a big shadow." ~ Swedish Proverb

Have you noticed that your child worries about new experiences, things changing, or the dangers of the world around them? Your reassurances may not help them calm down. **Worry** is an evolutionary function that gives us heightened alertness to environmental cues[28]. It can be useful in our lives if it helps us prepare well for a presentation or avoid entering the enclosure of the lion's den at the zoo. Remember that children's brains often cannot differentiate between a real threat and a perceived one. A task or a concept that may be difficult can resonate in their minds in the same way as an actual physical danger and produce that same "**fight, flight, freeze, flop**" response.

---

[28] Mathews, A. (1990). Why worry? The cognitive function of anxiety. *Behavior Research and Therapy, 28(6)*.445-468

As such, when worry grows to be so consuming that it becomes counterproductive in our personal lives, it can rise to the level of **anxiety**, which may require professional support. If we avoid all risks because we fear that something bad will happen, we (or our children) may miss all the fun! We want to encourage our children to try new things within reason. There are dangers in the world, but if we let our children become ruled by worry, they may miss a well-lived life.

My (Gayle's) youngest son began diving on a competitive team at seven. At that age, he was young enough to spend little time considering the dangers of flipping off a 3-meter diving board. By nine, he started to voice anxiety about going to practice, saying, "What if I get hurt? The dives they are asking me to do are too hard, and it makes me feel sick just thinking about it." As a parent, I had to consider whether he had stopped enjoying the sport or if anxiety was preventing him from taking pleasure in something he loved.

Together, my son and I investigated what anxiety felt like in the body - tight shoulders, an upset stomach, jitteriness, or even a headache - so that he could identify what was happening. We also discovered that people tend to focus better when they feel just a *little anxious*, and he admitted that diving requires a lot of focus to avoid belly-flopping - or worse! Over several months, my son started to see his worry as more of a *signal* that he needed to pay attention to what he was doing. This realization lowered his anxiety so that he still felt in control - and thus remained in control. Ultimately, he became a nationally-ranked diver at ten, so I am glad that we worked through his anxious feelings together so that he can now manage them himself. These newly developed skills of identifying worry/anxiety, investigating its root cause, and working through it, will serve him in other ways as he grows older.

"These newly developed skills of identifying worry/anxiety, investigating its root cause, and working through it, will serve him in other ways as he grows older."

Additionally, to continue to ease his anxiety and keep that newfound confidence going, my (Gayle) son and I did research into other famous divers, and found that the world-famous Olympic Gold Medalist Greg Louganis used his power of visualization to rehearse his dives mentally before he executed them physically. Much to the delight of my son, here was a world class athlete who used his strengths of visualization to his fantastic advantage - and my son identified with that! He was no longer anxious; he was eager to do the same - and it worked splendidly!

Another example of what we did to ease anxiety happened when I (Lin) began searching for a high school for my son, who has always struggled with transitions. We needed a plan when a school was chosen because my son was so anxious. We collaborated with administrators to scaffold the school trial day into small chunks of one class per day, spaced a few days apart, to allow my son time to process, adapt, and adjust to the changes. Although it took longer initially, what was gained was incredibly worthwhile: my son believed that the new school valued his input and would support him when needed. Because of his newfound trust, I have noticed that my son has become more open to trying new experiences in school.

> *"The more we know, the less fear of the unknown there is, and more often than not, anxiety is not much more than fear of the unknown."*

These are real life positive examples of how knowledge is our ally against anxiety. The more we know, the less fear of the unknown there is, and more often than not, anxiety is not much more than fear of the unknown. We are anxious because we don't know the outcome and cannot completely control it. Children inherently know this but often cannot articulate it. We must educate our children about what they are experiencing in these terms and show them that anxiety is surmountable by discussing the situation, deciding what you or your child can control, then finding tactics to strengthen their abilities to overcome their challenges.

What can you do when your child is worried? You can help your child identify the concern if they are able. If they are too young to tell you, ask them to point to where they *feel* worried or even draw a picture showing it. You can also observe when the anxious behaviors occur - during a specific time of day, around certain people, or in a particular environment. Note what those behaviors can look like - crying, clinging to a caretaker, or avoiding activities such as preschool. Your child may seem "out of sorts." An older child may complain about headaches, stomach upset, or seem moody or irritable. You might notice changes in eating or sleeping habits as well. Interestingly, studies have shown that children over seven were more able to link physical and emotional symptoms of anxiety[29], whereas younger children could only identify the physical symptoms.

29 Muris, P., Mayer, B., Freher, N. K., Duncan, S., & van den Hout, A. (2010). Children's internal attributions of anxiety-related physical symptoms: Age-related patterns and the role of cognitive development and anxiety sensitivity. Child Psychiatry and Human Development, 41(5), 535–548. doi.org/10.1007/s10578-010-0186-1

Muris, P., Vermeer, E., & Horselenberg, R. (2008). Cognitive development and the interpretation of anxiety-related physical symptoms in 4–13-year-old non-clinical children. *Journal of Behavior Therapy and Experimental Psychiatry*, 39(1), 73–86. doi.org/10.1016/j.jbtep.2006.10.014

Once you recognize that your child is struggling, help them identify their feelings about the stressor. Be an open, curious listener, reflecting back so they know that you hear what they are saying. Here are some things you might say to your worried child:

I'm right here with you. You are safe.

Everything is OK, this moment will pass.

Tell me what you think will happen next.

I get worried sometimes, too.

How can I help?

Let's take a moment to breathe.

Your soothing behavior will help to calm them when you have a close emotional bond. Share about a time when you were worried and how you worked through the challenge. Talk about how adults care for themselves and how children can do so. Show them how certain things may make us feel better, such as exercising[30], sleeping well[31], and doing things that we enjoy. Try a mindfulness[32] exercise together or list things you are grateful for in a journal[33]. These activities help to rewire the brain to be more oriented toward positivity.

We encourage you to use the books recommended below as conversation starters to discuss strategies and explore what might help your child. In *There's No Such Thing as a Dragon* by Jack Kent, a little boy recognizes that if he identifies his worries instead of ignoring them, he can live with them. Likewise, in *When Things Aren't Going Right, Go Left* by Marc Colagiovanni, a boy carries his worries in a backpack, putting them down when they no longer serve him. When young children can identify with the characters in a picture book, it will help them verbalize their feelings, and you can work through them together.

30 Carter, Pascoe, M., Bastounis, A., Morres, I. D., Callaghan, P., & Parker, A. G. (2021). The effect of physical activity on anxiety in children and young people: a systematic review and meta-analysis. *Journal of Affective Disorders, 285*, 10–21. doi.org/10.1016/j.jad.2021.02.026
Zhang, Li, W., & Wang, J. (2022). Effects of exercise intervention on students' test anxiety: A systematic review with a meta-analysis. *International Journal of Environmental Research and Public Health, 19(11)*, 6709–. doi.org/10.3390/ijerph19116709
31 Pires, Bezerra, A. G., Tufik, S., & Andersen, M. L. (2016). Effects of acute sleep deprivation on state anxiety levels: a systematic review and meta-analysis. *Sleep Medicine, 24*, 109–118. doi.org/10.1016/j.sleep.2016.07.019
32 Fumero, A., Penate, W., Oyanadel, C., & Porter, B. (2020). The effectiveness of mindfulness-based interventions on anxiety disorders. A systematic meta-review. *European Journal of Investigation in Health, Psychology and Education, 10(3)*, 704–719. doi.org/10.3390/ejihpe10030052
Norton, A., Abbott, M. J., Norberg, M. M., & Hunt, C. (2015). A systematic review of mindfulness and acceptance-based treatments for social anxiety disorder. *Journal of Clinical Psychology, 71(4)*, 283–301. doi.org/10.1002/jclp.22144
33 Petrocchi, N., & Couyoumdjian, A. (2016). The impact of gratitude on depression and anxiety: the mediating role of criticizing, attacking, and reassuring the self. *Self and Identity, 15(2)*, 191–205. doi.org/10.1080/15298868.2015.1095794

Tips to Grow On

Listen to your worried child and restate what was said. Your child needs to know that you understand without judging or immediately trying to solve the problem.

Good health habits will help all of us feel better - adequate sleep, nutritious food, and regular outside activity.

Anxiety can sometimes be reframed as a message to our body to pay attention in that moment.

Mindfulness and gratitude practices have been found to increase our happiness and to decrease worry.

Suggested Books to Read About Worry

The Boy Who Searched for Silence
by Andrew Newman (2016)

Key Issues: Anxiety

Summary: A boy searches for silence around him but cannot find it. He is disappointed until he realizes he can find silence within himself and take it wherever he goes.

Child Appeal: Beautiful story about how to find inner peace

A Case of the Zaps
by Alex Boniello and April Lavalle (2022)

Key Issues: Empathy, Big feelings

Summary: Pi, a young robot, develops a case of the Zaps when he hears about the upcoming school field trip. When he works up the courage to tell his parents, they take him to see Dr. Bleep Bloop, who reassures Pi and gives him strategies for managing the Zaps. Pi uses what he has learned and has fun on his field trip.

Child Appeal: Cool technology references; specific suggestions for anxiety

Catching Thoughts
by Bonnie Clark (2020)

Key Issues: Anxiety

Summary: A little girl starts to worry. Her worry grows until she realizes she needs to acknowledge it and find positive thoughts to replace her worries.

Child Appeal: Worry is personified as a gray balloon that grows and shrinks, depending on how much it is noticed.

The Circles All Around Us
by Brad Montague (2021)

Key Issues: Anxiety, Empathy, Leading with strengths

Summary: Small and big circles around us vary based on how well we know the people in our lives. As we widen our circle to include more people, we can positively impact our world.

Child Appeal: Beautiful reminder that we are all connected

Suggested Books to Read About Worry

Nope. Never. Not for Me!
by Samantha Cotterill (2019)

Key Issues: Anxiety, Rigidity

Summary: A little boy is afraid to try new foods, but when he takes it step-by-step with the help of his dinosaur, he learns that he can do it after all.

Child Appeal: Specific strategies used to try new foods

Shy
by Deborah Freedman (2016)

Key Issues: Anxiety

Summary: Shy hides in the pages of a book because he is so anxious about seeing the world and meeting others. A beautiful bird flies past, and he bravely leaves his home to follow the bird. He explores the world and, eventually, makes a new friend who enjoys reading books as much as he does.

Child Appeal: So creatively written; a surprise at the end

There's No Such Thing as a Dragon
by Jack Kent (1975)

Key Issues: Anxiety, Big feelings

Summary: Billy Bixbee awakens to find a small dragon in his bedroom. Billy's mom tells him there is no such thing as a dragon. As Billy ignores the dragon throughout the day, it grows bigger and bigger until the dragon picks up the house and carries it down the street. Eventually, Billy gives the dragon the attention it craves, and it shrinks back down to a much more manageable size.

Child Appeal: A wonderful metaphor for anxiety in the form of a dragon

This Beach Is Loud!
by Samantha Cotterill (2019)

Key Issues: Anxiety

Summary: A little boy is excited to go to the beach, but when he finally arrives, he realizes that the beach is crowded and loud, and the sand is scratchy and hot. His dad helps him relax, and they get lost in the fun of a memorable beach day together.

Child Appeal: Many kids can relate to sensory issues

Suggested Books to Read About Worry

When Things Aren't Going Right, Go Left
by Marc Colagiovanni (2023)

Key Issues: Anxiety, Big feelings

Summary: A boy having a bad day decides to go left because "nothing was going right." As he faces challenges, he leaves his worries, doubts, and frustrations behind, and his day turns around. He realizes he can manage these feelings as long as they do not get too big or overwhelming, but if they do, he can put them down for a while.

Child Appeal: Cleverly written and illustrated, worries are represented as a backpack to carry and put down

What if My Child Is a Perfectionist?

"Anyone who has never made a mistake has never tried anything new."
~ Albert Einstein

Have you ever noticed that your child hesitates or refuses to try new things? Often, it is because they are timid, cautious, or afraid to fail. We have worked with young children who fear creating a piece of art because it might not turn out as well as they see it in their mind's eye. We also know stressed-out, high-performing teenagers who miss school on test days because of headaches and queasy stomachs due to anxiety. They would rather avoid taking the test than earn a lower-than-perfect score. These negative "coping mechanisms" can start in early childhood. It is much easier to help a worried three-year-old make a new friend than to work with a lonely 15-year-old who is paralyzed with anxiety. Once habits are developed, they can be challenging to change, so we want to work on these skills early.

Perfectionism is the need to perform at a high level that may be unrealistically imposed by oneself or others[34]. This trait is often seen among gifted and 2e children because others have told them that they are smart, and in their minds, smart can equal high achievement or even perfection. Children with perfectionistic traits may avoid challenging activities, preferring instead to have easy success. They also tend to measure their self-worth based on their ability to perform successfully, so making mistakes is intolerable. In a recent study, perfectionistic high school students reported that they were more likely to choose what their parents wanted rather than make their own choices, their parents tended to model perfectionism, and they believed that they would receive harsh consequences for failure[35].

"This trait is often seen among gifted and 2e children because others have told them that they are smart, and in their minds, smart can equal high achievement or even perfection."

---

34 Rasmussen, K., & Troilo, J. (2016). "It has to be perfect!": The development of perfectionism and the family system. *Journal of Family Theory & Review, 8(2)*, 154–172. doi.org/10.1111/jftr.12140

35 Speirs Neumeister, K., Williams, K. K., & Cross, T. L. (2009). Gifted high-school students' perspectives on the development of perfectionism. *Roeper Review, 31(4)*, 198–206. doi.org/10.1080/02783190903177564

Performing at a high level or wanting to do something well is not inherently troublesome. Healthy perfectionism can be used to succeed in our chosen school or work domains. When this desire negatively impacts a child's life, it is a problem. When a child is missing fun activities, has a meltdown over a simple mistake, or refuses to try, it is our job as parents to help by showing them that no one and nothing is perfect.

When our children are young, we want to convey that making mistakes is a natural part of learning. We can model and teach healthy ways to react to, process, and take action when mistakes occur in our day-to-day lives. Let them see that mistakes are how we grow. When we respond positively to a child's mistakes, they will be more likely to learn from them[36]. In addition, if we pair our child's mistakes with gentle corrective feedback, they will more willingly engage in conversation to find a solution[37]. Also, help your child

---

[36] Grassinger, R., Scheunpflug, A., Zeinz, H., & Dresel, M. (2018). Smart is who makes lots of errors? The relevance of adaptive reactions to errors and a positive error climate for academic achievement. *High Ability Studies, 29(1)*, 37–49. doi.org/10.1080/13598139.2018.1459294

Soncini, A., Visintin, E. P., Matteucci, M. C., Tomasetto, C., & Butera, F. (2022). Positive error climate promotes learning outcomes through students' adaptive reactions towards errors. *Learning and Instruction, 80*, 101627. doi.org/10.1016/j.learninstruc.2022.101627

[37] Metcalfe, J. (2017). Learning from errors. *Annual Review of Psychology, 68*, 465-489.

lean into a **growth mindset**[38], the idea that hard work and dedication can help us improve our skills. This will teach your child **resilience**, the ability to do hard things, and work through challenges. All are important to become happy, successful adults.

Another point to consider is how we give praise. When complimenting your child, praise the effort and the journey, not just the final product. You might say, "I like how hard you worked on that painting." When you imply their painting is only worthy if it wins an award, you reinforce the belief that performance is the only thing that matters. This can lead to "**analysis paralysis**[39]" or **underachievement**[40]. A child may avoid starting something new for fear of failure or

---

38 Dweck, C. (2012). *Mindset: How you can fulfill your potential*. Constable & Robinson.
39 Kumari, S. S., Raja, B. W., & Sundaravalli, S. R. (2021). Analysis paralysis – The product of information explosion. *Annals of the Romanian Society for Cell Biology, 25(4)*, 4456-4458. proquest.com/scholarly-journals/analysis-paralysis-product-information-explosion/docview/2584784868/se-2
40 Steenbergen-Hu, S., Olszewski-Kubilius, P., & Calvert, E. (2020). The effectiveness of current interventions to reverse the underachievement of gifted students: Findings of a meta-analysis and systematic review. *Gifted Child Quarterly, 64(2)*, 132–165. doi.org/10.1177/0016986220908601

may only produce work half-heartedly to avoid the pressure of being perfect. "If I don't try, I can't fail." By the way, many important inventions were created from mistakes. Dr. Alexander Fleming accidentally discovered penicillin. Sticky notes were invented from failed attempts by researcher Spencer Silver to develop a strong glue for the aerospace industry. George De Mestral created Velcro after he noticed the burrs stuck to his dog's coat. Mistakes can be beneficial - and prove to be very profitable!

Our favorite book showing that mistakes can be turned into something wonderful is *Beautiful Oops!* by Barney Saltzberg. I (Gayle) recently worked with a little boy who was terrified of making mistakes. Max either refused to start an activity for fear of failing or crumpled up every drawing he started. For a seven-year-old boy, this was a problem. A teacher wisely

thought to share the story about "beautiful oops'" with him. After several readings, Max could name a "beautiful oops" when it appeared in his daily life and eventually could produce his own work without terror. That lesson stuck with me, demonstrating the power of a patient teacher and the impact of reading a well-chosen story.

Enjoy reading the recommended books below with your children, reminding them that it is okay to make mistakes, even preferable sometimes. We are our children's most significant role models. We want them to view us as relaxed, flexible adults who try our best in what matters.

"That lesson stuck with me, demonstrating the power of a patient teacher and the impact of reading a well-chosen story."

Tips to Grow On

 Perfectionism itself is not a bad thing. Healthy perfectionism can help us achieve. Unhealthy perfectionism may become self-limiting and should be addressed.

 Reinforce the idea with your young child that making mistakes is how we learn.

 Work on your own perfectionism, if that is your tendency, as we are our children's most influential role models.

 Encourage your child to adopt a growth mindset, the idea that our basic abilities and skills are not "fixed" but can be improved through dedication and hard work.

Suggested Books to Read About Perfectionism

Alexander and the Terrible, Horrible, No Good, Very Bad Day
by Judith Viorst (1972)

Key Issues: Perfectionism

Summary: Alexander's day is worse than not perfect. Everything he can imagine goes wrong, from falling in the mud to losing his best friend to discovering a cavity at the dentist. He even has to eat lima beans for dinner! Alexander realizes that despite all these things, tomorrow is a new day.

Child Appeal: All of us can relate to a tough day!

Beautiful Oops!
by Barney Saltzberg (2010)

Key Issues: Perfectionism, Rigidity

Summary: It's okay to make mistakes! This is a book full of examples of oops' that are changed into beautiful things - a fold in a page becomes a penguin beak, a spilled spot of paint is made into a picture of an elephant, and a tear in a page is a crocodile's smile.

Child Appeal: Hands-on book that shows us the beauty of mistakes

The Dot
by Peter H. Reynolds (2003)

Key Issues: Perfectionism, Empathy

Summary: Vashti knows she cannot draw in art class. When her teacher challenges her, she draws a dot on the page. She is asked to sign her work of art, and Vashti, the artist, is born. By the end, Vashti passes along her passion for art to someone else.

Child Appeal: Entertaining illustrations, engaging dialogue

The Girl Who Never Made Mistakes
by Mark Pett and Gary Rubinstein (2011)

Key Issues: Perfectionism

Summary: Beatrice Bottomwell never makes mistakes. Everything she does is perfect. One day, she makes a big mistake in front of everyone and learns that she can live and enjoy life more when she is not pressured to be perfect.

Child Appeal: Humorously shows the challenges of perfectionism

Suggested Books to Read About Perfectionism

Ish
by Peter H. Reynolds (2004)

Key Issues: Perfectionism, Empathy

Summary: Ramon is a boy who loves to draw. He draws feverishly until, one day, his older brother laughs at his work, undermining his confidence. Ramon is sad without his art until his younger sister convinces him to look at everything in a new-ish way. His confidence is restored, and he feels even better than before.

Child Appeal: Entertaining illustrations, multicultural characters, wonderful message

My Book of Beautiful Oops!
by Barney Saltzberg (2017)

Key Issues: Perfectionism, Rigidity

Summary: This board book encourages readers to turn oops' into beautiful mistakes. There are places to scribble, draw, and rip things to transform them into something new, reminding children that mistakes are okay.

Child Appeal: A do-it-yourself companion to *Beautiful Oops!*

Penelope Perfect
by Shannon Anderson (2015)

Key Issues: Perfectionism, Anxiety

Summary: Penelope is perfect in everything she does. When forced to have a less-than-perfect day, she feels relieved and learns she can relax and have fun while still doing her best.

Child Appeal: Relatable to all mini-perfectionists!

Rosie Revere, Engineer
by Andrea Beaty (2013)

Key Issues: Perfectionism, Leading with strengths

Summary: Rosie Revere loves to invent things. She works day and night creating new ideas until, one day, her uncle laughs at her creation. After that, Rosie keeps her inventions hidden to avoid any ridicule from others. Eventually, Rosie's aunt encourages her to invent something that flies. While her machine only flies for a second, Rosie learns that the only failure in life is when she fails to try.

Child Appeal: Inspiration for all young inventors!

Suggested Books to Read About Perfectionism

Perfect
by Max Amato (2019)

Key Issues: Perfectionism, Anxiety

Summary: An eraser is relieved when all the surrounding space on the page is neat and clean, but when a mischievous pencil makes a mark, a battle ensues between the eraser and the pencil. Ultimately, the eraser decides it is better to work with a friend than to be perfectly alone.

Child Appeal: Quirky characters, wonderfully illustrated

How Do I View My Child as a Whole Person?

"Today you are you, that is truer than true. There is no one alive who is youer than you." ~ Dr. Seuss

We are each a whole person, a sum of more than our parts, and we all have strengths and weaknesses. This is important to remember as we raise our children. It is easy for us to latch on to some aspect of our children, positive or negative, and use it to label them. My (Gayle) grandmother always said that my side of the family was musical and that the other side was artistic. Both are positive characteristics, but my aunt resented that she was not considered artistic and musical despite playing a musical instrument like her brother. My aunt felt pigeonholed as someone with only one talent instead of being known as the well-rounded person she was.

Imagine that a child is labeled with a negative trait, such as messiness. Each time the child spills something or ruins their clothes, they are labeled. After a while, the child will probably label themselves in their own minds. Children tend to believe what they are told, so, in fact, that messy toddler may become a teenager with an utterly unmanageable bedroom. *Why bother trying to be neat and organized when I am so messy? It's just how I am.* This leads back to our discussion in the previous chapter about having a growth mindset versus a fixed one. Providing a negative label for our child long enough may encourage the development of a fixed mindset - that a characteristic cannot be improved with care and effort. This does not sound like the way we want our children to view the world for a happy life.

Instead, let's consider that our children are living, breathing human beings with their own characteristics and preferences - apart from us. Just like all of us, they are multi-faceted and complex. They are often full of contradictions and inconsistencies. Your children might behave well, except when they are tired or hungry. They may build with blocks like a future engineer, but also equally love to kick a soccer ball around the backyard. They may spell well, but do not enjoy writing. They may love to crunch difficult math problems, as well as create a stunning piece of visual art. Similarly, your older child who reads way above their grade level still loves for you to read with them at the end of the day. Again, each child is different, so as responsive parents who are attuned to their individual needs, we need to see them as whole, unique people.

As we have explored various themes throughout this book, we cannot overemphasize the long-term impact of creating a safe and secure relationship with your child. A feeling of security can be developed as you explore high-quality books together during reading time. Developing a close bond with your child when they are young will pay off in spades in your child's teenage years. According to research, your older child's mental health may depend on it. Work to build the bond now!

Go forth and enjoy reading these creative, well-written books with your children. Listen carefully as they explore the themes that can be found in these stories: big feelings, managing worries, accepting differences in ourselves and others, wanting things a certain way, making mistakes, and learning about others' perspectives. As parents, we become the voice in their heads - so let's make it a positive one that allows them to see themselves through a healthy lens.

> *"As parents, we become the voice in their heads - so let's make it a positive one that allows them to see themselves through a healthy lens."*

Important Terms

Analysis Paralysis:
An inability to take action due to the overload of information and/or psychological, social, and/or physiological states

Anxiety:
An elevated state of heightened alertness to perceived danger

Asynchronous Development:
Occurs when a child is more developed in some ways and less in others

Co-Regulation:
When an adult helps soothe a child in times of stress

Deficits-Based Approach:
A perspective that focuses on what is "wrong" in order to "fix" a person

Empathy:
The ability to understand another's perspective which can also include experiencing another person's feelings and thoughts

Fight, Flight, Freeze, Flop Response:
Refers to our immediate, automatic, and instinctive responses to threats

Fixed Mindset:
Belief that one's abilities are unchangeable ("fixed") and/or something we are born with

Growth Mindset:
Belief that all abilities can grow through effort, repetition, and persistence

Outliers:
Anyone functioning outside of the normal range of abilities

Perfectionism:
Heightened standards of performance that may be imposed by the self or others

Resilience:
Capacity to work through challenges in a physically/mentally healthy manner

Role Model:
Someone who serves as an example of behaviors, goals, and/or beliefs for another person to identify and emulate

Self-Acceptance:
Being aware of and accepting who we are, including both positive and negative attributes

Self-Regulation:
Ability to manage one's thoughts and feelings in accordance with those in the surrounding environment

Sensory Differences:
When a person's five senses respond differently to external stimuli than others do

Strength-Based Perspective:
An approach that focuses on the positive aspects of a person or group, and encourages that person (or group) to develop those attributes

Underachievement:
A term used when performance is below expectations or predictions based on potential

Worry:
Thinking that is focused on preventing negative outcomes paired with negative feelings

About our Authors

Gayle Bentley M. M.Ed. is a doctoral student at Bridges Graduate School of Cognitive Diversity in Education and the mother of three amazing sons. She has taught instrumental music in the public schools for 23 years and now serves as the Gifted/2e Academic Director at 2e4ME Academy in Newport Beach, California. She is also the founder of The Bentley Center. She presents regularly at state and national conventions about giftedness and twice-exceptionality. Visit her website at *TheBentleyCenter.com*.

Dr. Lin Lim has a Ph.D. in human development psychology from Boston University, an Academic Graduate Certificate in twice-exceptional education from Bridges Graduate School of Cognitive Diversity in Education, and an Academic Graduate Certificate in Mind, Brain, and Education from Johns Hopkins University Graduate School of Education. She is a translational scientist specializing in sustainable well-being and complex outlier lifespan development through a dynamic systems perspective. Dr. Lim volunteers for gifted-related non-profits, currently serving on the board of Gifted Homeschoolers Forum (GHF), the PECAB advisory for the National Association of Gifted Children (NAGC), PGRetreat, and is the president of Supporting Emotional Needs of the Gifted (SENG). She is currently a Dean at Bridges Graduate School of Cognitive Diversity in Education and is pursuing an MBA at UCLA. She is an international presenter, author, creator of NEST!® and founder of the non-profit Quark Collaboration Institute Inc. Connect with her at *zenliving.com* & *Linkedin.com/in/linlimgoh*.

Printed in Poland
by Amazon Fulfillment
Poland Sp. z o.o., Wrocław